OXFORD GRADED READERS
750 HEADWORDS SENIOR LEVEL

More Funny Stories

by L. A. Hill

pictures by Joan Beales

1478
1978

OXFORD UNIVERSITY PRESS

Oxford University Press, Walton Street, Oxford OX2 6DP

OXFORD · LONDON · GLASGOW · NEW YORK · TORONTO · MELBOURNE
WELLINGTON · KUALA LUMPUR · SINGAPORE · JAKARTA · HONG KONG
TOKYO · DELHI · BOMBAY · CALCUTTA · MADRAS · KARACHI · IBADAN
NAIROBI · DAR ES SALAAM · CAPE TOWN

ISBN 0 19 421772 8

Printed and bound in England by
Hazell Watson & Viney Ltd, Aylesbury, Bucks

1 Jimmy was seven years old. He lived in the country, and he loved playing in the mud, but his mother did not like it, because he was always dirty, and he made the carpets dirty too. One morning he came home from the river. His legs were very muddy. His mother saw them and said, 'Go upstairs and wash your legs.' Jimmy went upstairs. Ten minutes later his mother went to the bottom of the stairs and shouted, 'Are your legs clean?' 'No,' Jimmy answered, 'but both of the towels are dirty now.'

2　Mr Jones had a nice, brown coat. He loved it very much, but his wife did not like it, because it was old. She often said, 'Give it to a poor man.' But Mr Jones always said, 'No, I like this coat.' Then a cigarette fell on it and made a hole in it, so Mrs Jones said, 'Please don't wear it again.' Mr Jones took it to a small tailor's shop and said to the tailor, 'Please make another coat like this one.' The tailor made the coat very carefully. Then he lit a cigarette, and made a hole in it in the same place.

3 Mr and Mrs Williams lived in a nice house in a small street in a town in England. Some new people bought one of the houses in their street. In the evening Mr Williams came home. His wife was at one of the windows of their living-room. 'Our new neighbours are very different from other people in this street,' she said. 'Oh?' Mr Williams said. 'How are they different?' 'They haven't got a radio,' Mrs Williams said, 'they haven't got a gramophone, they haven't got a car, and they haven't got any nice clothes.' 'Perhaps they prefer having some money,' her husband said.

4 Joan often ran around the house in her
nightdress in the evenings and mornings, but then
her mother said to her,' 'You're a big girl now,
Joan, and big girls don't run around the house in
their nightdresses.' That evening Joan put her
nightdress on again and ran into her brother's
bedroom. Her mother was downstairs in the
living-room, but she said, 'Joan, are you running
about upstairs in your nightdress again?' Joan
said, 'Yes, Mother, I am—but wait a minute.'
She ran into her bedroom, came out again a few
seconds later and shouted to her mother, 'I've taken
it off now!'

5 Two young women were neighbours, but they did not like each other very much. One day one of them visited the other. They drank coffee and talked about the weather, and then they began talking about babies. After a few minutes the first young woman went to a cupboard, took out a photograph of a young woman with a very pretty baby, brought it to her neighbour and said, 'Look at this. It's a photograph of me 22 years ago.' The other young woman looked at the photograph for a few seconds and then said, 'Oh? And who was the pretty baby?'

6   Mary was six years old. Her mother said, 'Mary, your grandmother's going to come and stay with us next week.'

Mary's grandmother arrived by air, and Mary and her mother went to the airport and met her. Mary's grandmother brought her some presents, and took her to the cinema.

Then Mary's mother said, 'Your grandmother's going back home tomorrow, Mary.' Mary was sad, because she loved her grandmother.

Mary and her mother went to the airport again. Her grandmother went to the aeroplane, and Mary began to cry. She said to her mother, 'Why does Granny live in the sky and not on the ground like everybody else?'

7   Mr and Mrs Jones had a drive in the country and saw an old woman there. She had some beautiful oranges. 'She's selling them very cheaply,' Mrs Jones said. Mr Jones stopped the car, and his wife got out and bought ten of the oranges. Then they talked to the woman. She said, 'Come and have tea with my husband and me in our house.'

They had some tea and cakes, and then Mrs Jones said to the woman, 'You sell your oranges very cheaply. Why do you do that?'

The woman smiled and said, 'We live in the country, and nobody lives near us. We like talking to people, but nobody stops here. Then we put those cheap oranges there, and now a lot of people stop. I bring them home, and we talk and we're happy.'

8 Mr Smith stayed in a small, cheap hotel for a few days, and then the man behind the desk in the hall said to him, 'Mr Smith, you've burned a hole in the table in your room with a cigarette. That's going to cost five pounds. Please give me the money.'

'Oh, no!' Mr Smith said. '*I* didn't burn your table. I don't smoke, and I've never had any cigarettes in my room.'

The man behind the desk said angrily, 'I've had this hotel for nearly twelve years now, and nobody has ever said, "I'm not going to pay for that burn" before!'

9   A young man met a pretty girl at someone else's house. He liked her very much and took her into the garden. They sat on a seat together, and the young man began boasting to the girl.

'I shoot a lot,' he said, 'and I make a lot of journeys too. A month ago I was in East Africa. I shot some lions, and then a big one jumped out at me from behind a bush. It was very quick, but I was quicker! I jumped into a river full of crocodiles and swam to the other side.'

'Oh?' the girl said kindly. 'I enjoy bathing too.'

10   Mr Miller went into a bar and sat down. There was another man in the room. He was in a corner. 'He's playing draughts,' Mr Miller thought. He looked—and then he looked again. 'That man isn't playing draughts with another man or a woman,' he thought. 'He's playing the game with a dog!' Mr Miller got up, went across the room and looked at the game. The dog did not play badly, but it lost. Then Mr Miller went to the man and said, 'Is that your dog?'

'Yes,' the man said.

'He's a very clever animal,' Mr Miller said.

'Oh, no,' the man said, 'he isn't very clever. I always win when we play draughts.'

11　Three prisoners met in a big camp in Russia. One of them said, 'The police sent me here because they said, "He is a friend of Strogoff's." I said, "But I have never met Strogoff! Who is he?" But they didn't listen, and they sent me here.'

The second prisoner said, 'The police sent *me* here because they said, "He is an enemy of Strogoff's." I too said, "I have never met Strogoff! Who is he?" But they sent me here too.'

Then the two prisoners looked at the third one and said, 'And why did they send *you* to this camp?'

The third prisoner said, 'I *am* Strogoff.'

12   Mr Williams had a lot of boats, and fishermen hired them from him. Mr O'Hara and his son Patrick hired one yesterday. They fished in several places, but caught nothing. Then they found a very good place, and caught about thirty fish there in an hour. Then it was late, and Mr O'Hara said, 'Row back to the beach now, Patrick.'

Patrick said, 'I'm going to come here again tomorrow.'

'Yes,' said his father, 'I'm going to too, but how are we going to find the place again?'

Patrick said, 'That's easy. Look! I've made a mark on the side of the boat.'

His father laughed and said, 'No, that's stupid! Mr Williams doesn't give us the same boat every time!'

13   Two boys had a fight in a village street. One of them stood near a tree and did not move his feet, and the other jumped about around him and hit him again and again because he did not move.

Several people came into the street and looked at the fight, and after a minute one of them said to the first boy, 'What are you doing, Joe? You're usually the fastest boy in the village. Why aren't you jumping about and hitting him a few times too?'

'Because we're fighting about 50p,' Joe shouted back, 'and I've got my foot on top of it!'

14   Mrs Jones was a teacher. Her house was not far from her school, and she always walked there in the morning. All the pupils in the school were very young. Mrs Jones walked to school on a very cold and windy morning in October, and the cold wind went into her eyes, and big tears began running out of them. She reached the school, opened the door and went into the hall. It was nice and warm there, and Mrs Jones was happy. But then a small boy looked at her for a few seconds, put his arm round her and said kindly, 'Don't cry, miss. School isn't *very* bad.'

15   Mrs Williams wanted a new hat. She saw one
in the window of a small, poor shop and liked it. She
went into the shop and said to the girl, 'I'm looking
for a hat. Please bring me that one out of your
window.' The girl went to the window, brought the
hat, and Mrs Williams put it on. Then she looked
around the shop for a mirror. There wasn't one. She
said to the girl, 'Haven't you got a mirror in your
shop?' 'No, we haven't,' the girl said. 'We had one,
but then we put it away, because ladies saw our hats
on their heads, and then they never bought them.'

16   Mrs Andrews was very fat. 'Don't eat bread or cakes,' her doctor said to her; and her husband said, 'I'm going to stop her eating them, doctor.'

Mrs Andrews made a beautiful cake, and her husband ate half of it. Then he went out, and his wife cut a very small piece and ate it. It was very good. She cut a bigger piece and ate that. In a few minutes she finished the cake. 'My husband's going to be very angry,' she said. 'What am I going to do?' She made another cake very quickly, ate half of that, and left the other half on the table. Her husband came back later, saw the half of the cake on the table and was quite happy.

17 Sally was five years old, and she began going to school. Her mother took her there in the morning, and in the afternoon she went there again and brought her home.

'Did you have a good time at school?' Sally's mother said to her.

'Yes,' the child said, 'it was nice.'

'What did you do?' her mother asked.

'We played games, and drew pictures, and sang some songs, and we had some milk, and then we had lunch.'

'Were the other children nice?' her mother asked.

'Yes,' Sally said, 'but there was a woman there, and I didn't like her because she talked all the time.'

18　Tom Davies was not old, but he did not have much hair. His wife Grace had thick, beautiful, black hair. Mr and Mrs Davies had one daughter. Her name was Jane, and she was four and a half years old. There was a photograph of her father in the living-room, and a few days ago Jane looked at it for a long time and then said to her mother, 'Mummy, why has Daddy got very little hair?'

Grace laughed and said, 'He's got very little hair because he thinks a lot Jane. He's a clever man.'

Jane looked at her mother's thick, black hair for a few seconds, and then she asked, 'Mummy, why have you got a lot of hair?'

19   It was Saturday, and Billy was not at school. He was at home. He went out into the garden in the morning and began playing. He played quietly for half an hour, but then there was a loud bang, and he began crying. He ran into the kitchen, and his mother was quite afraid. 'What have you done, Billy?' she said. 'Why are you crying? Did you fall down?'

'No, Mummy,' Billy said. 'I've broken Tiger's bowl.' Tiger was their old dog.

His mother put her arm round him and said, 'Don't cry about that, Billy. We've got other bowls in the house, and they're quite cheap. But how did you break that one?'

'I hit it with Daddy's new watch,' Billy said.

20 Some boys went for a holiday in the country and camped in a field near a river one afternoon. Then it began raining. It rained hard for two hours, and when it stopped, there was a lot of water in all the tents. One of the boys sat down on a box in his tent and began eating some bread and cheese. Then another boy came in. The first boy looked at the second boy's feet and then said to him, 'Please don't walk in this water with those dirty boots! We're going to sleep in it tonight.'

21   A lady went to her doctor and said to him,
'*I'm* quite well, doctor, but my son isn't. He loves
playing with mud, and he sometimes puts it in his
mouth and eats it.' She began to cry.

The doctor got up and put his hand on the lady's
arm. 'Don't cry about that,' he said to the lady
kindly. 'A lot of children eat mud for a few years,
and then they stop. Don't worry about it. Your son's
like lots of other children.'

'It doesn't worry you, doctor,' the lady said, 'but it
worries me a lot—and it worries my son's wife too.'

22   Molly's parents took her to the seaside for a
holiday last summer. The weather was hot, and
Molly liked ice-creams very much. Her parents took
her to the shops every morning for a walk, and they
always bought her an ice-cream. Then they went to
the beach for a bathe.

There was a wide road above the beach, and there
was a small wall at the side of it. Molly liked sitting
on the wall and eating her ice-cream and looking at
the people in the sea. But once some people were on
the beach under her, and a piece of her ice-cream
fell on one of them. He looked up and saw a big bird
in the sky above him.

'Do those birds live in refrigerators?' he asked
angrily.

23 Mrs Thompson was an important lady. She came to a small town for a holiday, and a journalist went to her hotel and talked to her. 'I'm going to write about you in our newspaper,' he said to her.

The journalist often talked to important people, because a lot of them came to his town for a holiday. He always said to the ladies, 'Have you ever found a man under your bed?'

When he said this to Mrs Thompson, she laughed and said, 'Yes, I have. Once a thief got into our house at night.'

'And you found him under your bed, did you?' the journalist asked. 'What did you do then?'

'I didn't find the *thief* under my bed,' Mrs Thompson said. 'I found my *husband* there.'

24   A man bought some cheap rings from a big shop and then began selling them in the street. 'Rings! Beautiful rings! Twenty-five pence each!' he said, but most of the people in the street were men, and none of them stopped. Then an old woman walked past slowly.

'I've got some nice rings here,' the man said to her. 'Twenty-five pence each. They're cheap.'

The old woman was deaf and did not hear him, but she stopped, went back and looked at some of the rings. Then she said to the man, 'How much are these rings?'

'Fifty pence each,' the man said loudly.

25   Mr Matthews was in a train, and he lost his
ticket. He looked in all his pockets, but it was not
there. There was another man in the same
compartment, and Mr Matthews said to him, 'I've
lost my ticket.'

The other man said, 'Where are you going?'

'To York,' Mr Matthews said.

The man got up and opened the door of the
compartment.

'Where are you going?' Mr Matthews said.

'I'm going to get you another ticket,' the man
said. He went out and closed the door.

He came back a few minutes later and gave Mr
Matthews a ticket for York.

'How did you get it?' Mr Matthews asked.

'It was quite easy,' the other man said. 'I went
into each compartment and said, "Are there any
tickets for York?", and a lady gave me this one.'

26   Miss Evans lived in a big city, and she had a very clever dog. She sent it to a good school in the country. After a few months it came back for the summer holidays, and Miss Evans said to it, 'What did you study at your school?'

'We studied English, arithmetic, history and foreign languages,' the dog said, 'and we played football.'

'And were you a good pupil?' Miss Evans asked.

'I wasn't very good at arithmetic and history,' the dog said, 'but I was very good at foreign languages and football.'

'That's good,' Miss Evans said. 'Now please say something to me in a foreign language.'

The dog said, 'Meow, meow!'

27 Captain Grey's old servant left, and a new one arrived and began working for him. On the first morning, this man cleaned the shoes and then brought Captain Grey one black shoe and one brown one. Captain Grey put the brown one on, and then he looked at the black one, and said to the new servant, 'But these shoes aren't a pair. Look at them! One of them's black, and the other's brown.'

The servant looked at the shoes for a few seconds and then said, 'Yes, you're quite right, Captain. And there's another pair like these in the cupboard. One of those is black too, and the other's brown.'

28 Bill and Ben were drunk. They got on to a bus, and Bill said, 'I'm going to buy the tickets,' but Ben said, 'No, I'm going to buy them.' He pushed Bill into a seat.

There was another man near the back of the bus. His clothes were blue. Ben went to him and said, 'Two tickets to Gosport Bridge, please.'

But the man did not take Ben's money. He said to him angrily, 'Don't give that to me. I'm a naval officer.'

Ben looked at the man for a few seconds and then shouted to his friend, 'Come here, Bill! We're going to get out of here! We've made a mistake! This isn't a bus. It's a ship!'

29   Fred was a soldier. He went to Singapore, and then his girl-friend sent him a letter. She lived in England, and she wrote, 'I'm not going to marry you when you come home, Fred. Please send my photograph back to me.'

Fred was angry. He went round all of his friends and asked them for photographs of their old girl-friends. Then he sent all of them to *his* girl-friend with *her* photograph and a short letter. He wrote in it, 'I've got a lot of girl-friends, and I've forgotten your face. I'm sending you photographs of all my girl-friends. Please keep yours and send the others back to me.'

30 Johnnie was four and a half years old. Last
week his mother said to him, 'Johnnie, I'm going to
take you to Edinburgh tomorrow. We're going to go
there in a big train.'

Johnnie and his mother went to the station and
got into the train. Their journey began, and Johnnie
was very happy. There were not many people in the

train, and Johnnie ran about, and played, and enjoyed everything.

But then the train went into a long tunnel. Johnnie was afraid. He sat down quickly and waited.

Then the train came out of the tunnel, and the sun shone in through the windows again. Johnnie laughed. 'Look, Mummy!' he said. 'It's tomorrow!'

31 Mr Mills wanted some furniture. He went into a shop and said, 'I want that furniture, but I haven't got much money.'

The man in the shop said, 'Pay us £20 now and take the furniture. Then pay us £5 each week for a year.'

Mr Mills was happy. He paid the man £20 and took the furniture. Then he paid £5 each week for two months, but after that he stopped.

One or two weeks later he got a letter from the furniture shop. It asked for the money.

Mr Mills wrote back, 'Your letter of 26th March about furniture never reached me, because I do not live at this address any more.'

32   A farmer brought a sack of money into his
bank and said, 'I've got some money here. Please
put it in your bank. There are £11,000 in this sack.'

The bank clerk was very surprised and said,
'Counting all this money's going to take a long
time. Please come back in an hour.'

The farmer left the bank and went out shopping
with his wife. They came back after an hour, and the
clerk said to them, 'There are £11,050 in your sack,
not £11,000. Several of us have counted it, and we
all say the same.'

The farmer turned to his wife and said, 'There! I
told you! You put the wrong sack in the car!'

33 A woman was at the cinema, and she was
enjoying the film very much, but there was a man in
the next seat, and he began looking on the floor
under him. The woman was angry and whispered,
'What are you doing there? What are you looking
for?'

'A piece of hard chocolate,' the man whispered to
her. 'I've dropped it on the floor.'

'A piece of chocolate?' the woman said angrily.
'It's dirty now! Take this and be quiet, please! I'm
listening to the film!' She gave the man a big piece
of chocolate.

'But,' the man said, 'my teeth are in the piece on
the floor!'

34 Mr Thomas came home from work early yesterday evening. His wife was usually in the kitchen at that time, but that evening she was not. Mr Thomas went upstairs and opened the door of the living-room. His wife was on the floor there, and there was a man near her head. He had something heavy in his hand. Mr Thomas was afraid. 'What are you doing?' he said to his wife and the man. Mrs Thomas laughed and said, 'Don't be afraid, George. This man's going to paint the ceiling of our living-room next week. He's brought several tins of paint and put some of each colour on the ceiling, and I'm lying on the floor and looking at them and choosing one of the colours.'

35 Mrs Green lived in a quiet village. Last week she visited her old aunt. She lives near a big town, and there is a wide road behind her house. There are always lots of cars, buses and trucks in this road, and they drive very fast.

At half-past eleven Mrs Green was on one side of the road, and her aunt's house was on the other side. Mrs Green began crossing the road several times, but then she always ran back again, because more cars, buses and trucks came towards her very fast.

There was another woman on the other side of the road. She looked at Mrs Green for a few minutes, and then she smiled at her.

Mrs Green smiled too and then shouted to her, 'How did you get across the road?'

The other woman laughed and shouted back, 'I didn't! I was born on this side!'

36   Mr Peters wears glasses. A few weeks ago he went to the zoo near his town. He saw a lot of people round one of the cages. They were laughing. Mr Peters went to the cage. There were some nice monkeys in it. Mr Peters went nearer the cage. Then he saw a small notice on the bottom of it. He went very near and put his head down.

Then one of the monkeys came to the front of the cage, put a hand out, took Mr Peters's glasses, put them on its face and jumped up on to a rope.

All the people round the cage laughed loudly. Mr Peters put his face very near the notice and read, 'THESE MONKEYS TAKE GLASSES'.

37 Mr Brown had an umbrella shop in a small town. People sometimes brought him broken umbrellas, and then he took them to a big shop in London. The people in the shop mended the broken umbrellas, and then Mr Brown went and took them back to his shop.

A few weeks ago he went to London by train. He did not have an umbrella that day, but there was another man in the seat in front of him, and he had an umbrella.

The train reached London, and Mr Brown and

the other man stood up. Mr Brown took the other man's umbrella, because he usually had one during his trips by train. But the other man said angrily, 'That's my umbrella!' Mr Brown gave it to him.

Then he went to the big shop. They had six umbrellas for him. He looked at each of them and then said, 'You've mended them very well.'

In the afternoon he went to the station and got into the train again. The same man was in the same seat. He looked at Mr Brown and his six umbrellas. 'You've had a good day,' he said.

38 Mr Andrews took his wife to a restaurant yesterday evening. They sat down, but the restaurant was very full, and none of the waiters came to their table.

Mr Andrews was angry. He said, 'I'm tired and hungry. I want my food.'

He went out of the restaurant and found a telephone. He telephoned the restaurant and said, 'My wife's at a table in your restaurant. She's wearing a red hat.'

The waiter went into the dining-room and looked at the people there. Then he went to the telephone again and said to Mr Andrews, 'Yes, she's here. Do you want her?'

'No, I don't,' Mr Andrews said, 'but she hasn't got any food, and she wants some. She's hungry.'

Then he went into the restaurant again. There was a waiter at his table now, and Mr Andrews was happy.

2 **tailor:** tailors make coats and trousers.

4 **nightdress:** women and girls wear nightdresses in bed.

6 **Granny:** grandmother. Children usually say, 'Granny', but older people usually say 'Grandmother'.

8 **burn:** We burn wood and coal on our fires. This cigarette is burning the table. The cigarette made this burn on the table.

9 **boast:** Small boys sometimes say, 'I'm very good at swimming (or running, or fighting).' Then they are boasting.

crocodile: This is a crocodile. Crocodiles live in rivers in Africa and Asia.

10 **draughts:** These people are playing draughts.

think/thought: This man is talking. This man is not talking. He is thinking. He thought yesterday too. We think in our heads, but we do not say anything.

11 **prisoner:** This man is a prisoner.

12 **hire:** Mr Williams has bought a boat. He has given £100 for it. Now it belongs to him. But Mr O'Hara has hired a boat. He has given £2 for two hours. After two hours he is going to give it back again.

mark: This boy has made a mark on that wall with some paint.

place: This cat has found a warm place near a fire. These boys are going to play football. This is a good place.

13 **move:** This boat is not moving, because there isn't any wind. But now it's moving fast, because there's a lot of wind.

14 **tear:** There are tears on this woman's face. Tears come out of your eyes when you cry.

15   **mirror:** This woman is looking in a mirror.

     saw: We see with our eyes. We saw with our eyes yesterday.

19   **bang:** Guns and bombs make a loud bang, and then our ears sometimes hurt.

21   **worry:** 'Don't worry' = 'Don't be sad and afraid.' 'It worries me' = 'It makes me sad and afraid.'

22   **refrigerator:** We put food in our refrigerator, and then it is cold. We make ice and ice-cream in refrigerators too. This is a refrigerator.

23   **important:** The man in the middle of this picture is an important person.

     journalist: Journalists write things in newspapers. That is their work.

24   **deaf:** This man is deaf. His ears are not good.

     hear: We hear with our ears. Deaf people do not hear very well.

25 compartment: There are eight compartments in this carriage.

27 pair: A pair of shoes is one left shoe and one right shoe. A pair of horses is two horses.

28 drunk: These men have drunk a lot, and now they are drunk. They are very happy, or very sad, or they fight, or they go to sleep.

naval: This man is an army officer. And this man is a naval officer.

29 girl-friend: Maisie is a girl, and she is Fred's friend. We say: 'Maisie is Fred's girl-friend.'
tunnel: A tunnel is a hole through the ground. This is a tunnel.

31 **pay/paid:** 'Pay us £20 = 'Give us £20 for something.' 'He paid £20' = 'He gave £20 for something.'

32 **farmer:** Farmers have land and fields and cows. They work on their land, and sell milk, cows and vegetables.
sack: This is a sack.

surprised: This woman is surprised and happy because her husband has given her some flowers. She is surprised because he does not often give her any. This man is surprised and angry, because someone has taken his car.

33 **chocolate:** This is a piece of chocolate. Chocolate is sweet and brown.

whisper: speak very quietly.

34 **choose:** This man is going to buy his wife a new dress. There are three dresses here, and the man is going to buy one of them. His wife is going to choose one. She is going to say, 'I want this one,' or 'I want that one.'

paint: This man is painting a wall. It was white, but now it is going to be black, because he is painting it with black paint.

36 **notice:** This is a notice.

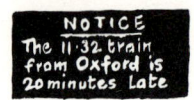

37 **mend:** There is a hole in this sock. This woman is mending it now.

38 **restaurant:** This is a restaurant. People eat in restaurants.

waiter: This man is a waiter. He brings food to people in restaurants.